*Presented to:*_____

*Given by:*_____

*Date:*_____

DATE DUE	

Ten-digit ISBN: 0-8054-3176-4
Thirteen-digit ISBN: 978-0-8054-3176-6

Published by Broadman & Holman Publishers,
Nashville, Tennessee

Dewey Decimal Classification: 248.84
Subject Heading: CHRISTIAN LIFE—HUMOR

The quoted ideas expressed in this book (but not Scripture verses) are not, in all cases, exact quotations, as some have been edited for clarity and brevity. In all cases the author has attempted to maintain the speaker's original intent. In some cases quoted material for this book was obtained from secondary sources, primarily print media. While every effort was made to ensure the accuracy of these sources, the accuracy cannot be guaranteed.

Scripture quotations are taken from: The Holy Bible, New International Version (NIV), copyright © 1973, 1978, 1984, by International Bible Society; New King James Version (NKJV), copyright © 1979, 1980, 1982, Thomas Nelson, Inc., Publishers; New American Standard Bible (nasb), © the Lockman Foundation, 1960, 1962, 1963, 1968, 1971, 1972, 1973, 1975, 1977; used by permission; New Living Translation (NLT), copyright © 1996. Used by permission of Tyndale House Publishers, Inc., Wheaton, Illinois 60189. All rights reserved; New Century Version (NCV), © 1987, 1988, 1991 by Word Publishing, Dallas, Texas 75039, and used by permission; *The Message*, the New Testament in Contemporary English © 1993 by Eugene H. Peterson, published by NavPress, Colorado Springs, Colo.; The Holman Christian Standard Bible™ (HCSB), copyright © 1999, 2000, 2001 by Holman Bible Publishers, used by permission; and King James Version (KJV).

1 2 3 4 5 6 7 8 9 10   10 09 08 07 06 05

Dr. Swan's

Prescriptions for

Parent-itis

Dennis Swanberg

and CRISWELL FREEMAN

BROADMAN
&HOLMAN
PUBLISHERS

NASHVILLE, TENNESSEE

℞

Dedicated to
parents who cherish
their kids and
the Father

Contents

A Few Words from The Swan

ello! I'm Dennis Swanberg, also known as "The Swan." Perhaps you've seen me on television, or maybe you've heard me speak in person. Or maybe you just picked this book up because you're an interested parent who wants to learn more about the vitally important job of raising children in this difficult world. In writing this book my purpose was simple: to make you chuckle a little—and think a lot—about the important job of parenting.

If you're a momma or a daddy, you probably don't need anybody (including The Swan) to tell you that the task of raising your kids is both incredibly challenging *and* incredibly rewarding. And to help you in that task, I've decided to define a new diagnosis called "Parent-itis." Here's my definition:

> Parent-itis: a condition that results from the job of being a loving, caring parent; symptoms may include: sleepless nights, worried minds, dwindling bank accounts, messy houses, unmade beds, smudgy carpets, empty gas tanks, sticky tabletops, unfolded laundry, frequent visits to the pediatrician, full grocery carts, and empty refrigerators. Parent-itis results in increased obligations (and stress) during the following times: Christmas, Easter, Halloween, Valentine's Day, all other major holidays, birthdays, weekends, school days, afternoons, and all days that end in the letter y.

In addition to the above symptoms, those who contract Parent-itis also receive massive quantities of love, appreciation, admiration, affirmation, and satisfaction. In summary, Parent-itis is both an obligation *and* a gift, with the value of the gift far outweighing the cost of the obligation.

I know about Parent-itis from firsthand experience. I watched and learned plenty about parenting from my mom and dad: Pauline Bernadeen (that's my Momma) and Floyd Leon (that's Daddy Dear with two capital *D*s). They both had periodic attacks of Parent-itis because of me! Despite my imperfections, my parents were world-class, God-fearing folks who served as a marvelous example. Next I got a firsthand dose of Parent-itis by helping my gorgeous wife Lauree raise two wonderful boys: Chad and Dusty. The boys are just about as good as boys can be, but they can still drive you a little crazy at times. So there you have it: I've had plenty of experience with Parent-itis without ever leaving the friendly confines of the Swanberg clan. But there's more.

God called me to the ministry, and for twenty years I had the privilege of being a pastor. During that time I had the honor of counseling plenty of parents on the joys and duties of being fully involved in a loving Christian family. I saw lots of couples who made family life a pleasure, and more than a few who didn't. Along the way I made careful mental and emotional notes about the differences between the families that flourished and the ones that floundered. And this book is a result of the things I've learned.

These pages can serve as timely reminders of the things you'll need to do and the words you'll need to speak in order to help your children grow to be responsible, godly adults.

If you're a loving parent who feels overwhelmed from time to time, welcome to the club. And if you'd like a treasury of time-tested ideas that can help you do a better job raising those beautiful babies and terrific teenagers of yours, this book can help. The concepts in this book aren't new, but they are powerful *if* you use them.

So take a prescription from The Swan: read this book from cover to cover, and do everything you can to follow the advice that you find in it. When you do, you'll find a cure for Parent-itis, and while you're at it, you'll enjoy some of the greatest joys this side of heaven.

Chapter 1

A Case of Parent-itis

Insanity is hereditary; you get if from your children.

—

Sam Levenson

Hi Mom and Dad,

Are you feeling "charming, chipper, cheery, and chirpy"? Or are you too pooped to pop *and* too tired to care? Your answer may have something to do with whether or not you have young kids in the house. If you're an empty-nester with lots of retirement money and nobody to spend it on, you've probably picked up the wrong book. Or, if you're a perfect parent with perfect kids living in a perfect home (complete with a perfect dog, a perfect cat, and a perfect parakeet), then do yourself a favor: don't change a thing. But if you're like the rest of us, you probably have the normal pressures that most of us moms and dads face from time to time. I call it Parent-itis. Here's how you know if you've got it:

1. You've probably got a case of Parent-itis if . . . you're a loving parent who's temporarily worn out, stressed out, and pooped out (but hopefully not yet *passed* out!).
2. You've probably got a case of Parent-itis if . . . you're overworked, underfunded, and overcommitted (but hopefully not yet "officially" committed!).

3. You've probably got a case of Parent-itis if . . . your heart is full and your bank account isn't.

4. You've probably got a case of Parent-itis if . . . you spend approximately half of your disposable income at the grocery store, but you still don't have anything in the house that your kids want to eat.

5. You've probably got a case of Parent-itis if . . . you constantly find yourself saying the words to *your* teenagers that your parents said *to you* when *you* were a teenager (and yes, ladies, despite your deepest fears, you *are* becoming your mother and I'm becoming Floydish!)

If you've got Parent-itis, don't hit the panic button or the eject button—in fact, do just the opposite: say a word of thanks to the Great Big Parent upstairs. Why? Because the fact that you've got Parent-itis means that you've got kids who love you and depend on you. And that makes you a lucky person indeed.

Your kids, troublesome though they may sometimes be, are God's gift to you. This book is intended to help you nurture that gift in ways that are pleasing to God and helpful to your children.

Even on those difficult days when the house is in an uproar, the laundry is piled high—and the bills are piled even higher—wise parents never forget their overriding goal: shaping young minds and hearts. The very best parents shape those minds with love, with discipline, and with God. And the ideas in this book can help you do precisely that.

So with no further ado, let's celebrate God's blessings . . . starting, of course, with the children that He has, in His infinite wisdom, entrusted to your care.

A hundred years from now it will not matter what my bank account was, the sort of house I lived in, or the kind of car I drove. But the world may be different because I was important in the life of a child.

Kathy Davis

The darn trouble with cleaning the house is it gets dirty the next day anyway; so skip a week if you have to. The children are the most important thing.

Barbara Bush

℞ When my kids become wild and unruly, I use a nice, safe playpen. When they're finished, I climb out.

Erma Bombeck

℞ Next year five million kids will turn sixteen, and ten million parents will turn pale.

Before I got married, I had six theories about
bringing up children: now I have
six children and no theories.

John Wilmot

When you have children, it is not enough to put a
roof over their heads, food in their bellies, braces
on their teeth, stereo headphones in their ears,
$35 jeans on their bodies, and combs in their back
pockets. You also have to DO things with them.

D. L. Stewart

The best time for parents to put the children to
bed is while they still have the strength.

Herman Phillips

Most things have an escape clause,
but children are forever.

Lewis Grizzard

Raising children requires courage,
not to mention a sense of humor.

Liz Curtis Higgs

There are three ways to get something done:
Do it yourself; hire somebody to do it; or tell
your kids they *can't* do it.

Anonymous

Parents: persons who spend half their time
worrying how a child will turn out, and the rest of
the time wondering when a child will turn in.

Ted Cook

Rx
Raising Kids...
takes a big one to
raise one.

You really believe in heredity when your child's
report card is all As.

Anonymous

The accent may be on youth, but the
stress is still on the parents.

Anonymous

Consider the lilies of the field. Look at the fuzz on
a baby's ear. Read in the backyard with the sun on
your face. Learn to be happy. And think of life as a
terminal illness because, if you do, you will live it
with joy and passion, as it ought to be lived.

Anna Quindlen

R̆ You know you're a
parent when . . . you
seriously begin pondering
the question "Peter Pan
or Skippy"?

Prescriptions from Above . . .

About Our Children

The righteous man walks in his integrity; His children are blessed after him.

Proverbs 20:7 NKJV

Teach a youth about the way he should go; even when he is old he will not depart from it.

Proverbs 22:6 HCSB

I have no greater joy than to hear that my children walk in truth.

3 John 1:4 KJV

Train up a child in the way he should go, and when he is old he will not depart from it.

Proverbs 22:6 NKJV

Dr. Swan's Prescriptions for Parent-itis

Don't panic . . . just persevere and pray: If your kids are driving you crazy, don't, for a minute, think that all is lost. And whatever you do, don't lose hope; just trust your instincts, trust God even more, and keep looking for solutions. And while you're looking for solutions, keep praying for your kids; . . . *they* need your prayers almost as much as *you* need the experience of praying for them.

Be consistent: Of course your child's behavior will upset you from time to time, but your love for them should never be in question. A parent's love must never be turned on and off like the garden hose; it should, instead, flow like the mighty Mississippi, too deep to touch bottom and too strong to stop.

Let home be a happy place: Home should be a refuge for the relaxed. Let a lot of "the stuff" go! Love everyone unconditionally! 'Cause remember . . . you need it too!

Don't be too hard on yourself: You don't have to be a perfect parent to be a godly one. Do the best you can, and leave the rest up to God.

Remember: Laughter is good medicine: Milton Berle said, "Laughter is an instant vacation." And when you laugh with your family, it's an instant *family* vacation.

Chapter 2

We're All Teachers

Every home is a school. What are you
going to teach today?

—

Marie T. Freeman

I f you're a parent in our twenty-first-century world, you
need keen insight, prudent foresight, and sharp eyesight.
But that's not all. You also need discipline, patience,
prayer, and a willingness to teach.

Parents are their kids' most important instructors. Daniel
Webster wrote, "If we work in marble, it will perish; if we work
upon brass, time will efface it; if we rear temples, they will
crumble into dust; but if we work upon immortal minds and
instill in them just principles, we are then engraving upon
tablets which no time will efface, but which will brighten and
brighten to all eternity." These words remind us of the glori-
ous opportunities that are available to those of us who teach
our children well.

I learned about the power of parental examples from two of
the finest parents this old world has seen since Adam and Eve
decided to tie the knot. My Momma, Pauline Bernadeen
Swanberg, was grace! And my Daddy, Floyd Leon Swanberg,
was the law! But in reality Mom and Dad were both reservoirs

of mercy and love. Our family was faith, work and love. And in the midst of it all, life was fun. Life was simple, not so much stuff, just real relationships. Mom and Dad had grown up in the country—and took their country values to the city. My sisters and I grew up with the best of both worlds: the farm and the new family thing called a subdivision. We weren't white collar—more blue collar—not quite ring around the collar. And that's why I know that my role as a teacher can have a profound impact on my two boys, Chad and Dusty.

Are you and your spouse teaching from the same curriculum? And does that curriculum begin and end with *the* Book. Hopefully so, because that's exactly what your children need.

Do you sincerely seek to leave a lasting legacy for generations to come? If so, you must start by teaching your children the ways and the Word of God. And remember always that your most enduring lessons are not the ones you teach with words; they are the ones you teach by example. When you obey God's commandments and trust His promises, your life will be a shining lesson for *your* children . . . and *for theirs*.

No matter what, Dad was always there with solid words of advice . . . "Go ask your mother."

Alan Ray

You cannot teach a child to take care of himself unless you will let him try. He will make mistakes; and out of these mistakes will come his wisdom.

Henry Ward Beecher

Not only should we teach values, but we should live them. My kids pay a lot more attention to what I do than what I say. A sermon is better lived than preached.

J. C. Watts

America's future will be determined by the home and the school. The child becomes largely what it is taught; hence, we must watch what we teach it and how we live before it.

Jane Addams

℞ You know you're a parent when . . . you finally stop criticizing the way your parents raised you.

At home the young child has opportunities to
watch and learn from a variety of models
who make learning enjoyable. Success brings a hug
or sometimes a snack. Also, the
student-teacher ratio is low.

Joe Nathan

That which we are we are all the while we're
teaching—not voluntarily but involuntarily.

Ralph Waldo Emerson

Training is not telling, not teaching, not
commanding, but something higher than all of
these. It is not only telling a child what to do,
but it is also showing him how to do it and
seeing that it is done.

Andrew Murray

"Suzanne will not be at school today," I once wrote
to her teacher. "She stayed at home to play with
her mother." I don't remember many other days of
her elementary years. But I remember that day.

Gloria Gaither

R̥ You know you're a parent when . . . your kid's playroom has more moving parts than the space shuttle.

Their little minds had a thousand hands reaching and grabbing for everything they could see (not unlike their physical hands). A parent-teacher's job is to guide as much as possible what the hands of their minds grab and store.

Beth Moore

For three years I felt like all I did was pick up toys, coordinate naps, and kiss boo-boos. But I began to realize that there was a whole other level to my life and that I'd never had a more important job: I was teaching my children how to respond to God.

Lisa Whelchel

℞ You know you're a father when . . . the day that your teenage daughter announces that she's going out on her first date, you decide to put the whole family in the Witness Protection Program.

My heart's desire is to find more opportunities to give myself away and teach my children the joy of service at the same time.

Liz Curtis Higgs

We always need to be on the lookout for those teachable moments with our children— spontaneous lessons that appear in the side yard, the laundry room, and the grocery store.

Susan Card

The time for teaching and training is preteen. When they reach the teenage years, it's time to shut up and start listening.

Ruth Bell Graham

Prescriptions from Above . . .

About Teaching Our Children

Listen, my son, to your father's instruction and do
not forsake your mother's teaching.

Proverbs 1:8 NIV

Teach [My words] to your children, talking about
them when you sit at home and when you walk
along the road, when you lie down and when you
get up. Write them on the doorframes of your
houses and on your gates, so that your days and the
days of your children may be many in the land
that the LORD swore to give your forefathers.

Deuteronomy 11:19-21 NIV

Wise people's minds tell them what to say, and
that helps them be better teachers.

Proverbs 16:23 NCV

Teach me Your way, O LORD;
I will walk in Your truth.

Psalm 86:11 NKJV

Dr. Swan's Prescriptions
for Parent-itis

Teaching takes time: Helping our children understand the fundamental truths of Christian living requires a lot of time. Our children are always learning. As parents, we must ensure that they are learning from us.

Self-control at school starts at home: Teachers can certainly help, but we cannot expect them to retrain our children. When it comes to the importance of self-control, we, as parents, must be the ones to teach our kids how to behave. We need to behave better than the kids and that's not easy!

Familiarize yourself with the opportunities of tomorrow: The world of tomorrow is filled with opportunities for those who are willing to find them and work for them. Make certain that you have more than a passing familiarity with the ever-shifting sands of our changing America. Then share your insights with the young people who live under your roof.

Talk things over: If your child has done something that is impulsive, discourteous, or dangerous, your natural response will be anger. But as soon as you calm down, help your child learn from the experience by talking about the behavior, its motivations, and its consequences. Social skills are special keys to success!

Chapter 3

The Right Kind of Example

Parents can tell—but never teach—until they
practice what they preach.

—

Anonymous

I t would be *very* easy to teach our kids everything they need
to know about life *if* we could teach them with words alone.
But we can't. Our kids hear some of the things we say,
but they watch *everything* that we do. They have their own
built-in "candid camera"!

What kind of example are you? Are you the kind of parent whose life serves as a powerful example of righteousness?
Are you a parent whose behavior serves as a positive role
model for your youngsters? Are you the kind of parent whose
actions, day in and day out, are based upon integrity, patience,
fidelity, and a love for the Lord? If so, you are not only blessed
by God; you are also a powerful force for good in a world that
desperately needs positive influences such as yours.

As parents, we serve as unforgettable role models for our
children and our grandchildren. The lives we lead and the

choices we make should serve as enduring examples of the spiritual abundance that is available to all who worship God and obey His commandments.

Are you God's obedient servant? Is your faith in Christ clearly demonstrated by the example that you set for your children? If so, you will be blessed by God, and so, of course, will they.

Phillips Brooks advised, "Be such a man, and live such a life, that if every man were such as you, and every life a life like yours, this earth would be God's paradise." And that's sound advice because our families and friends are watching . . . and so, for that matter, is God. So, smile . . . you're on your loved ones' "candid camera"!

> The most effective way for parents to command obedience is by a clean, pure, wholesome Christian example.
>
> *Billy Graham*

Be an organ donor—give your heart to Jesus!

More depends on my walk than my talk.

D. L. Moody

Be sure that you first preach by the way you live. If you do not, people will notice that you say one thing but live otherwise, and your words will bring only cynical laughter and a derisive shake of the head.

Charles Cardinal Borromeo

Nothing speaks louder or more powerfully than a life of integrity.

Charles Swindoll

We must mirror God's love in the midst of a world full of hatred. We are the mirrors of God's love, so we may show Jesus by our lives.

Corrie ten Boom

Preach the gospel everyday; if necessary, use words.

St. Francis of Assisi

Among the most joyful people I have known have been some who seem to have had no human reason for joy. The sweet fragrance of Christ has shown through their lives.

Elisabeth Elliot

A child identifies his parents with God, whether adults want the role or not. Most children "see" God the way they perceive their earthly fathers.

James Dobson

Of all commentaries on the Scriptures, good examples are the best.

John Donne

While my father could not compel me to be a Christian, I had no choice because of what he did for me and what I saw in him.

G. Campbell Morgan

Setting an example is not the main means of influencing another; it is the only means.

Albert Einstein

Children have more need of models than critics.

Joseph Joubert

The power of example in a parent does more to train a child than any other single thing.

Larry Christenson

℞ Your example is a language that any kid can read—especially your kid.

What you do speaks so loudly that
I cannot hear what you say.

Ralph Waldo Emerson

I don't care what a man says he believes with his
lips. I want to know with a vengeance what he
says with his life and his actions.

Sam Jones

If a child sees his parents day in and day out
behaving with self-discipline, restraint, dignity,
and a capacity to order their lives, then the child
will come to feel in the deepest fibers of his being
that this is the way to live.

M. Scott Peck

℞ If you can't be an "Onward Christian Soldier," at least don't pass the ammunition to the enemy.

Prescriptions from Above . . .

About Being a Good Example

Be an example to the believers in word, in
conduct, in love, in spirit, in faith, in purity.

1 Timothy 4:12 NKJV

You are the light of the world. A city situated on a
hill cannot be hidden. No one lights a lamp and
puts it under a basket, but rather on a lampstand,
and it gives light for all who are in the house.
In the same way, let your light shine before men,
so that they may see your good works and give
glory to your Father in heaven.

Matthew 5:14-16 HCSB

Set an example of good works yourself, with
integrity and dignity in your teaching.

Titus 2:7 HCSB

I have given you an example to follow.
Do as I have done to you.

John 13:15 NLT

Dr. Swan's Prescriptions
for Parent-itis

Mirror, mirror, on the wall, who's the biggest role model of all? When you look into the mirror, you're gazing at the person who is the primary role model for your child. It's a big responsibility, but you and God are up to it!

Language 101: Unfortunately, your children will grow up in a crude, profanity-laced world. Help set the right example by choosing your words with care.

When you make a mistake, admit it: No parent is perfect, not even you. Consequently, you will make mistakes from time to time, and when you do, set the proper example by apologizing to the offended party, especially if that party is related to you by birth.

Living your life and shining your light . . . on your children: As a parent, the most important light you will ever shine is the light that your own life shines on the lives of your children. Make your light shine brightly, righteously, obediently, and eternally!

Chapter 4

The Honor of Being an Honorable Parent

I'd rather be the man who bought the Brooklyn
Bridge than the man who sold it.

—

Will Rogers

When you're an honorable parent, you give your child a gift that money can't buy. Charles Swindoll correctly observed, "Nothing speaks louder or more powerfully than a life of integrity." Wise parents agree.

What lessons about honor did you learn from your childhood? And are you living in accordance with the lessons that you learned?

It has been said on many occasions and in many ways that honesty is the best policy. For believers it is far more important to note that honesty is *God's* policy. And if we are to be servants worthy of Jesus Christ, we must be honest and forthright in our communications with others. Sometimes honesty is difficult; sometimes honesty is painful; sometimes honesty is inconvenient; but honesty is always God's commandment.

In the book of Proverbs, we read, "The LORD detests lying lips, but he delights in men who are truthful" (12:22 NIV).

Clearly, we must strive to be parents whose words are pleasing to our Creator. Truth is God's way, and it must be our way, too, even when telling the truth is difficult. As loving parents, we should do no less—indeed we *must* do no less.

> Truth is like the cork: however often
> submerged it rises again.
>
> *Ivan Panin*

> Character is formed by doing the thing we are
> supposed to do, when it should be done, whether
> we feel like doing it or not.
>
> *Father Flanagan*

> Let your tongue speak what your heart thinks.
>
> *Davy Crockett*

℞ If you're an honorable parent, you'll make your kid as proud and happy as an ant in a cookie factory.

℞ *Beware of half-truth; you may get ahold of the wrong half.*

Ability may take you to the top, but it takes
character to keep you there.

John Wooden

What could be more important than equipping the
next generation with the character and
competence they need to become successful.

Colin Powell

The mind of Christ is to be learned in the family.
Strength of character may be acquired at work, but
beauty of character is learned at home.

Henry Drummond

If you "made it wrong" . . . by God's grace,
"make it right"!

The Swan

℞ **Those who stretch the truth usually find that it snaps back.**

Let God use times of waiting to mold and shape your character. Let God use those times to purify your life and make you into a clean vessel for His service.

Henry Blackaby and Claude King

To let oneself be bound by a duty from the moment you see it approaching is part of the integrity that alone justifies responsibility.

Dag Hammarskjöld

Pride opens the door to every other sin, for once we are more concerned with our reputation than our character, there is no end to the things we will do just to make ourselves "look good" before others.

Warren Wiersbe

Prescriptions from Above . . .
About Integrity

As for you, if you walk before me in integrity of heart
and uprightness, as David your father did, and do all
I command and observe my decrees and laws, I will
establish your royal throne over Israel forever, as
I promised David your father when I said, "You shall
never fail to have a man on the throne of Israel."

1 Kings 9:4–5 NIV

For this very reason, make every effort to
supplement your faith with goodness, goodness
with knowledge, knowledge with self-control, self-
control with endurance, endurance with godliness.

2 Peter 1:5–6 HCSB

The integrity of the upright will guide them, but
the perversity of the unfaithful will destroy them.

Proverbs 11:3 NKJV

Let integrity and uprightness preserve me,
for I wait for You.

Psalm 25:21 NKJV

Dr. Swan's Prescriptions for Parent-itis

Discuss the importance of integrity: Teach the importance of integrity every day, and, if you run out of lessons to teach, use words.

Display integrity in matters both great and small: Right is right and wrong is wrong whether the issue appears large or inconsequential. And when it comes to issues of integrity, you are a twenty-four-hour-a-day example to your child, so be on guard.

When the truth is hard for parents: Telling the truth isn't just hard for kids; it can be hard for parents too. And when honesty is hard, that's precisely the moment when wise parents remember that their children are watching . . . and learning.

If your child tells a falsehood, talk about it: Even "little white lies" are worthy of a parent-to-child talk; the bigger the lie, the bigger the talk.

Chapter 5

Laughter Is the Best Medicine

He who laughs lasts—he who doesn't, doesn't.

—

Marie T. Freeman

Healthy relationships include laughter. Every relationship, whether it is with your spouse, your kids, or your coworkers, can be filled with joy and with laughter. Laughter, as the old saying goes, is medicine for the soul. But sometimes, amid the stresses of the day, we forget to take our medicine. Instead of viewing our world with a mixture of optimism and humor, we allow worries and distractions to rob us of the joy that God intends for our lives.

If you're suffering from the inevitable demands of twenty-first-century parenting, or if you've got a full-blown case of Parent-itis, you know all too well that a good laugh may seem as scarce as hen's teeth. But it need not be so. And if you're having trouble getting your funny bone in gear, here's a helpful hint from your old pal The Swan: LIGHTEN UP AND DON'T TAKE THINGS SO SERIOUSLY (especially yourself). When you do, you'll soon learn that everything goes better when you learn to laugh at yourself *and* when you learn to find humor in life's little mishaps.

Your life is either a comedy or a tragedy, depending upon how you look at it. Make yours a comedy. So today, as a gift to yourself, to your spouse, and to your kids, approach life with a smile on your lips and a chuckle in your heart. After all, God created laughter for a very good reason . . . and since the Father knows best, you might as well laugh while you can.

We are here just for a spell and then pass on. So get a few laughs and do the best you can. Live your life so that whenever you lose, you are ahead.

Will Rogers

The most wasted of all days
is one without laughter.

E. E. Cummings

The day returns and brings us the petty round of irritating concerns and duties. Help us perform them with laughter and kind faces; let cheerfulness abound with industry.

Robert Louis Stevenson

Laughter is the shortest distance
between two people.

Victor Borge

Genuine wisdom is knowing that rest is rust, and
that real life is in love, laughter, and work.

Elbert Hubbard

Humor is a prelude to faith, and laughter
is the beginning of prayer.

Reinhold Niebuhr

Trouble knocked on the door, but,
hearing a laugh within, hurried away.

Ben Franklin

Laughter is the sun that drives winter
from the human face.

Victor Hugo

R You know you're a
parent when . . . your
favorite comic actor
in a starring role is
Scooby Doo.

A keen sense of humor helps us to overlook the
unbecoming, understand the unconventional,
tolerate the unpleasant, overcome the unexpected,
and outlast the unbearable.

Billy Graham

To me, a healthy belly laugh is one of the most
beautiful sounds in the world.

Bennett Cerf

Laugh and the world laughs with you.
Weep and you weep alone.

Ella Wheeler Wilcox

A good laugh is sunshine in the house.

William Makepeace Thackeray

R̸

Laughs: Use 'em or lose 'em.

℞ If you can't laugh at yourself, don't worry . . . other people are bound to do it for you.

Laughter dulls the sharpest pain and flattens out the greatest stress. To share it is to give a gift of health.

Barbara Johnson

I think everybody ought to be a laughing Christian. I'm convinced that there's just one place where there's not any laughter, and that's hell.

Jerry Clower

There is nothing that rejuvenates the parched, delicate spirits of children faster than when a lighthearted spirit pervades the home and laughter fills its halls.

James Dobson

If there is laughter in the home . . . your loved ones will return to say "there's no place like home."

The Swan

Eight Ways to Know You're a Parent
You Know You're a Parent If . . .

1. Your idea of fine dining is a Happy Meal that's super-sized.

2. You count the sprinkles on each kid's cupcake to make sure they're equal.

3. Your vote for "Man of the Year" is Barney.

4. You buy ketchup in half-gallon containers.

5. You can name all four characters on Teletubbies . . . *and* their birthdays.

6. The outside of your car is cleaner than the inside.

7. You actually think the North Pole was discovered by Dora the Explorer.

8. You can't remember whether the hero of *Moby Dick* was Captain Ahab, Captain Kangaroo, or Captain Crunch.

Prescriptions from Above . . .
About Laughter

There is a time for everything, and everything
on earth has its special season. There is a time
to cry and a time to laugh. There is a time
to be sad and a time to dance.

Ecclesiastes 3:1, 4 NCV

A merry heart makes a cheerful countenance.

Proverbs 15:13 NKJV

A happy heart is like good medicine.

Proverbs 17:22 NCV

Oh, clap your hands, all you peoples! Shout to
God with the voice of triumph!

Psalm 47:1 NKJV

This is the day the LORD has made;
we will rejoice and be glad in it.

Psalm 118:24 NKJV

Dr. Swan's Prescriptions for Parent-itis

Get everybody laughing: If family life is the cake, then laughter is the icing. And everybody in your clan deserves a slice with *lots* of icing. And its OK to lick the leftover icing from the bowl.

Laughing at somebody isn't usually very funny . . . Unless that somebody is yourself!

When it comes to humor, don't say anything you wouldn't want God to hear . . . Because He will. God loves heartfelt laughter *if* it's for the right reasons. Select your jokes, pranks, and stories accordingly.

If you can't see the joy and humor in everyday life, . . . you're not paying attention to the right things. Remember the doughnut-maker's creed: "As you travel through life brother, whatever be your goal, keep your eye upon the doughnut, and not upon the hole."

Chapter 6

Time, Time, and More Time

Children spell "love": T-I-M-E.

—

Anthony P. Witham

I t takes *lots* of time to build a strong bond between a parent and a child. So do yourself *and* your child a favor: forget about trying to squeeze in a few minutes here or there and calling it "quality time." When it comes to your family, you'll have a hard time getting *quality* if you don't insist upon *quantity* too.

Every child is different, but every child is similar in this respect: he or she wants and needs *plenty* of family time (whether he or she is willing to admit it or not). And make no mistake—parents (unlike you) who try to "farm out" their kids to the care of "hired hands" are making a big mistake. So here's a tip from The Swan to mommas and daddies everywhere: don't delegate your kids.

Healthy families don't just spring up overnight like those darned dandelions in my front yard; healthy families are built year by year, day by day, moment by moment. And the responsibility of building any family lies squarely on the shoulders of the parents. Responsible parents take ample time to share, to care, to watch, to listen, and to teach their kids. Irresponsible parents let the world shape their kids' minds and hearts . . . and everybody suffers.

What kind of time are we talking about? Time spent at church. Time spent at ball games. Time spent in bull sessions. Time spent on vacations. Time spent doing yard work. And chores around the house. Time spent at the dinner table; time spent in the car; time spent watching (a few) good, clean shows on TV. Responsible parenting is about time, time, and more time.

Do you want to be the kind of parent that your kids deserve? Then give them plenty of time—*your* time. Don't be satisfied to give your kids the scraps that are left from the main course of your day. Give your children a heaping helping of honest-to-goodness, fully involved, nondiluted, pure, 100 percent time. Accept no substitutes—because your kids won't.

R̥ The best thing to spend on your children is time.

Bulletin Board Blooper:

The eighth-graders will be presenting Shakespeare's *Hamlet* in the church basement on Friday at 7 p.m. The congregation is invited to attend this tragedy.

There's no doubt about it: children are expensive little people. To raise them properly will require the very best that you can give of your time, effort, and financial resources.

James Dobson

There is nothing more special, more precious than time that a parent spends struggling and pondering with God on behalf of a child.

Max Lucado

I have decided not to let my time be used up by people to whom I make no difference while I neglect those for whom I am irreplaceable.

Tony Campolo

R A child is someone who stands halfway between an adult and a TV set.

When parents have time for their kids, when they get together almost every day for conversation and interaction, then their teens do much better in school and life.

James Dobson

Prime-time parents are parents who consider every minute with their children a prime time to communicate the message of parental love, interest, and care.

Kay Kuzma

When we love something, it is of value to us; and when something is of value to us, we spend time with it, time enjoying it, and time taking care of it. Got a minute? So it is when we love children: we spend time admiring them and taking care of them. We give them our time.

M. Scott Peck

I don't buy the cliché that quality time is the most important thing. If you don't have enough quantity, you won't get quality.

Leighton Ford

Many things we need can wait. The child cannot. Now is the time his bones are being formed; his blood is being made; his mind is being developed. To him we cannot say tomorrow. His name is today.

Gabriela Mistral

To those who would say, "We don't have time o do these things!" I would say, "You don't have time not to!"

Stephen Covey

R̥

Time is not recyclable.

℞ To be in your children's memories tomorrow, you have to be in their lives today.

Children desperately need to know—and hear in ways they understand and remember—that they're loved and valued by Mom and Dad.

Gary Smalley and John Trent

When children know they are valued, then they feel valuable.

M. Scott Peck

It is not a slight thing when they, who are so fresh from God, love us.

Charles Dickens

The soul is healed by being with children.

Fyodor Dostoevsky

Prescriptions from Above . . .

About the Gift of Time

To everything there is a season, a time for every purpose under heaven.

Ecclesiastes 3:1 NKJV

℞

Prescriptions from Dr. Swan

Listen with your ears, your eyes, and your heart. And remember: Wise parents pay careful attention to the things their children don't say.

Dr. Swan's Prescriptions for Parent-itis

Taking time *and* making time for family: How much time should you dedicate to your family? The answer is straightforward: You should invest *large quantities* of high-quality time in caring for your clan. As you nurture your loved ones, you should do your very best to ensure that God remains squarely at the center of your family's life. When you do, He will bless you in ways that you could have scarcely imagined.

Meaningful moments in small packages: You don't have to haul your kid to a deserted island to have a meaningful conversation. Meaningful moments between you and your child can happen anywhere—and it's up to you to make sure that they do.

Quality versus quantity: Can every single moment spent with your family be "high quality"? No way. Time comes in many flavors: high quality, medium quality, low quality, and "I-wish-I-could-forget-that" quality. But if you're a responsible parent, things will eventually even out. In other words, if you spend enough quantity time with your loved ones, the quality will eventually take care of itself.

Chapter 7

Church and the Drug Problem

My Parents Drug Me to Church;
Your Kids Need to be Drug Too

—

Dr. Swan

When I was growing up, my parents drug me to the Baptist church every time the doors opened (or so it seemed to me at the time). And come to think of it, I'll have to admit that I wasn't always thrilled about going. On those sunny summer days when the church was hot and the preacher was not, I longed to be somewhere—*anywhere*—but church. But my parents made me go anyway.

Today, as I look back on my childhood, I am profoundly grateful that my folks hauled me to church as often as they did. It gave me a clear understanding of the importance of worship. And that's a lesson that all Christian parents should be teaching their children.

As families, we can't *not* worship. We may think that we can skip church and still worship God on Easter and Christmas, . . . but we really can't do it. If we're not worshipping God 365 days a year, we're worshiping something else.

And when we worship *anything* besides God, that's a problem . . . a BIG problem. That's why we, as responsible Christian parents, must do our part by dragging our kids—whether the little angels like it or not—to church.

When we lead our families to church faithfully each Sunday, we are blessed. But if we don't darken the doors of the church for months at a time, we forfeit countless spiritual blessings that might otherwise be ours.

So, if you're a concerned Christian parent (and because you're reading this book, I strongly suspect that you are), here's a tip: make regular worship an ironclad, no-excuses-allowed habit. Your kids deserve no less . . . and neither, for that matter, do you.

R̟ Don't wait for six strong men to haul you into church.

Our churches are meant to be havens where the caste rules of the world do not apply.

Beth Moore

R

Home improvement:
Take your family to
church.

The church is where it's at. The first place of Christian service for any Christian is in a local church.

Jerry Clower

Every time a new person comes to God, every time someone's gifts find expression in the fellowship of believers, every time a family in need is surrounded by the caring church, the truth is affirmed anew: the Church triumphant is alive and well!

Gloria Gaither

The church is not a museum for saints but a hospital for sinners.

Morton Kelsey

Going to church is never up for discussion or a vote. We're all going!

Floyd Leon Swanberg

R Christians are like coals of a fire. Together they glow— apart they grow cold.

The church needs people who are doers of the
Word and not just hearers.

Warren Wiersbe

Christian brotherhood is not an ideal which we
must realize; it is rather a reality created by God in
Christ in which we may participate.

Dietrich Bonhoeffer

Be united with other Christians. A wall with
loose bricks is not good. The bricks must
be cemented together.

Corrie ten Boom

The Bible knows nothing of solitary religion.

John Wesley

One of the ways God refills us after failure is
through the blessing of Christian fellowship.
Just experiencing the joy of simple activities
shared with other children of God can
have a healing effect on us.

Anne Graham Lotz

And how can we improve the church? Simply and
only by improving ourselves.

A. W. Tozer

One's home is his castle, but one's
"church home" is his mansion.

The Swan

R A cold church is
like cold butter . . .
it doesn't
spread well.

Some people are so busy observing ritual that
they never get to know God personally. Ritual
must bring me to close personal contact
with God, or it's useless.

Grady Nutt

Worship is your spirit responding to God's Spirit.

Rick Warren

Don't ever come to church without coming
as though it were the first time, as though it
could be the best time, and as though it
might be the last time.

Vance Havner

R

Parents, be the
soul support of
your children.

Prescriptions from Above . . .
About Church

Now you are the body of Christ,
and individual members of it.

1 Corinthians 12:27 HCSB

For we are God's fellow workers; you are God's
field, you are God's building.

1 Corinthians 3:9 NKJV

Therefore take heed to yourselves and to all the
flock, among which the Holy Spirit has made you
overseers, to shepherd the church of God which
He purchased with His own blood.

Acts 20:28 NKJV

And I say also unto thee, That thou art Peter, and upon
this rock I will build my church; and the gates of hell shall
not prevail against it. And I will give unto thee the keys
of the kingdom of heaven: and whatsoever thou shalt bind
on earth shall be bound in heaven; and whatsoever thou
shalt loose on earth shall be loosed in heaven.

Matthew 16:18–19 KJV

For where two or three come together in my name,
there am I with them.

Matthew 18:20 NIV

Dr. Swan's Prescriptions for Parent-itis

Don't drop them off: If church is good enough for your kids, it's good enough for you too. So set the right example by attending church *with* your family.

Forget the excuses: If somebody starts making up reasons not to go to church, don't pay any attention . . . *even* if that person is you!

Not just on Sundays: Teach your kids that worship isn't just for Sunday mornings. Demonstrate to your family that worshipping God is a seven-day-a-week proposition, not a one-day-a-week intermission.

Make it a celebration, not an obligation: Your attitude towards church will help determine your kid's attitude toward church . . . so celebrate accordingly! His house is fun!

Chapter 8

Living the Truth . . . and Nothing but the Truth

I was walkin' in the cemetery with my wife to get
some ideas for a tombstone. I came upon one that
said, "Here lies an honest man and a politican.
I said, "How about that dear, two men
buried in the same grave."

—

The Swan

Face it: Your kids have a built-in baloney detector. If you try to teach them to do one thing while you're doing the opposite, they'll figure out pretty quickly that your words are *pure* baloney. As the old saying goes, you can't kid a kid.

So here's a question: Are the words that come out of your mouth the same ones that reside in your heart? If so, you're on the right track. But if you find yourself occasionally pretending to be someone you're not, God wants to have a little chat with you.

Other people may hear your words—and other people may be fooled by those words for a little while—but God sees the heart. And if you allow anything besides God to reign over your heart, you're inviting trouble into your own life *and* into the lives of your loved ones.

Whether you realize it or not, you are a powerful example for your children to follow. And whether you realize it or not, your family is learning far more from the life you live than from the words you say. This raises an important question: what sort of example are you? Are you the kind of believer whose words and deeds are consistent? And do those words and deeds honor the One who gave His life on a cross so that you might enjoy life eternal? Hopefully so!

As you encounter the challenges of everyday living, you will have many opportunities to serve as an enduring example of righteousness. Seize those opportunities now because your family is carefully watching—and constantly learning.

> ℞ Usually, the truth doesn't break until it's been thoroughly stretched.

God doesn't expect you to be perfect, but he does insist on complete honesty.

Rick Warren

Those who walk in truth walk in liberty.

Beth Moore

Truth will triumph. The Father of truth will win, and the followers of truth will be saved.

Max Lucado

Begin very early to instruct a child on the true values of life: love for all mankind, kindness, integrity, trustworthiness, truthfulness, and devotion to God.

James Dobson

℞ Our habits become our kids' habitats for their humanity—you didn't know your were building a habit for humanity did you?

R If you want to teach family values, try using fewer lectures and more visual aids.

We must learn, then, to relate transparently and genuinely to others because that is God's style of relating to us.

Rebecca Manley Pippert

Character is made in the small moments of our lives.

Phillips Brooks

Every time you refuse to face up to life and its problems, you weaken your character.

E. Stanley Jones

A real Christian is the one who can give his pet parrot to the town gossip.

Billy Graham

Prescriptions from Above . . .

About Living Honestly

Lead a quiet and peaceable life in all
godliness and honesty.

1 Timothy 2:2 KJV ·

The man of integrity walks securely, but he who
takes crooked paths will be found out.

Proverbs 10:9 NIV

A truthful person will have many blessings, but
those eager to get rich will be punished.

Proverbs 28:20 NCV

These are the things you are to do: Speak the truth
to each other, and render true and sound judgment
in your courts.

Zechariah 8:16 NIV

Teach me Your way, O LORD;
I will walk in Your truth.

Psalm 86:11 NASB

Dr. Swan's Prescriptions for Parent-itis

Live according to the principles you teach: The sermons you live are far more important than the sermons you preach.

They can read your mind: Kids (and spouses) are amazingly sensitive. So be careful with your thoughts as well as your actions.

Do the right thing: If you're constantly misbehaving, how can you expect your kids not to.

We are all a work in progress: Have a healthy vulnerability with your loved ones. We are all on a journey of growth. Practice mercy and grace . . . and make sure you're progressing.

When angels fall . . . If you make a mistake, apologize immediately. And if your child makes a mistake, help your child understand why the behavior is wrong and how to prevent it in the future.

Chapter 9

Education and Wisdom

The only thing more expensive than education is ignorance.

—

Ben Franklin

When it comes to educating your kids, it's best to turn everything over to the "experts," right? Wrong! When it comes to educating that little boy or girl who lives under your roof, it's up to *you* to decide what's right and what's not. Responsible parents (like you) should do the same thing Harry Truman did; they should put a sign on the desk that reads, "The Buck Stops Here."

No teacher on earth can possibly know as much about your child as you do. And no teacher on earth can possibly have the same impact on your child as you will. So, when all is said and done, no teacher (or school) should be expected to take the responsibility for educating your little angel. That responsibility, dear Mom and Dad, is yours. And make no mistake: it's a *big* responsibility.

The old familiar song praises the value of "readin' and writin' and 'rithmetic." And it still applies. Every child deserves an early exposure to the joys of reading, and every child deserves an education in the basics of grammar and mathematics. When we allow our children to pass through the halls of academia without a firm grasp of "the fundamentals," we do them a profound disservice—but there's more.

Every child also deserves extensive training in character-building: lessons about honesty, responsibility, discipline, attitude, courtesy, dignity, self-worth, and respect for others. Certainly those lessons can and should be taught in school, but the ultimate training ground should be the home.

Responsible parents understand the value of education. Children often do not. That's why it's up to us, as the grown-ups in the family, to stress the importance of education. Here in the twenty-first century, education is no longer a luxury. It is a powerful tool and a shining light that snuffs out the darkness of ignorance and poverty. And when it comes to education, your child deserves nothing but the best.

When I was a boy of fourteen, my father was so
ignorant I could hardly stand to have him around.
But when I got to be twenty-one, I was astonished
at how much he had learned in seven years.
Mark Twain

Education is not given for the purpose of earning
a living; it's learning what to do with a living
after you've earned it.
Abraham Lincoln

The doors of wisdom are never shut.

Ben Franklin

The growth of the human mind is still
high adventure, in many ways the highest
adventure on earth.

Norman Cousins

Children are sponges. Other's actions are absorbed.
Is the water clean?

David Ian Gussin

The truly human society is a learning society,
where grandparents, parents, and children are
students together.

Eric Hoffer

**A child's education should
begin at least a hundred years
before he is born.**

Oliver Wendell Holmes Sr.

R̲

If you lack knowledge, go to school. If you lack wisdom, get on your knees.

Vance Havner

The primary values, attitudes, skills, and competencies that my children will grow up with will be learned—or not learned—in my home.

Tim Hansel

Kids' "social studies" will be handy some of the time, but their "social skills" will be useful *all* of the time!

The Swan

Lessons learned at mother's knee last through life.

Laura Ingalls Wilder

The place for a child to learn religious faith is at home, with family, where faith is lived and practiced.

Dick Van Dyke

Spiritual training should begin before children can even comprehend what it is all about. They should grow up seeing their parents on their knees before God, talking to Him. They will learn quickly at that age and will never forget what they've seen and heard.

James Dobson

What children learn at home is what they will take with them when they are grown.

Chuck Christensen

Is your child learning of the love of God through your love, tenderness, and mercy?

James Dobson

You can lead a boy to wonder, but you can't make him think.

Mary T. Freeman

I am always sorry to hear that a person is going to school to be educated. This is a great mistake. If the person is to get the benefit of what we call education, he must educate himself, under the direction of the teacher.

Fanny Jackson Coppin

Education is hanging on until you've caught on.

Robert Frost

Enter school to learn; depart to serve.

Mary McLeod Bethune

Education does not develop your character until it merges with integrity and wisdom.

Sam Nunn

Prescriptions from Above . . .
About Learning and Wisdom

Commit yourself to instruction; attune your ears to hear words of knowledge.

Proverbs 23:12 NLT

A wise man will hear and increase in learning, and a man of understanding will acquire wise counsel.

Proverbs 1:5 NASB

Give instruction to a wise man, and he will be still wiser; teach a just man, and he will increase in learning.

Proverbs 9:9 NKJV

Listen, my son, to your father's instruction and do not forsake your mother's teaching.

Proverbs 1:8 NIV

Every morning he wakes me. He teaches me to listen like a student. The Lord God helps me learn.

Isaiah 50:4–5 NCV

Dr. Swan's Prescriptions for Parent-itis

Stress the importance of learning: Some families stress the importance of education more than other families. Make yours a home in which the importance of education is clearly a high priority.

Don't bad-mouth the school system: If you don't respect your kid's teacher, how can you expect your kid to? If you, as a parent, have a problem with a teacher, talk to the teacher (not the student). And when it comes to your child's school, be a booster, not a critic.

Be a participating parent: Let your child *and* you child's teachers know that you're available, responsive, helpful, and involved.

Remember: It's worth it. Face it—getting your kid through school is *expensive* in terms of time and money. But remember this: the value of a good education far outweighs its cost.

Chapter 10

Teenagers and Other Mysteries of Life

Family life got better, and we got our car
back—as soon as we put "I Love Mom"
on the license plate.

—

Erma Bombeck

I f you're a parent of a perfect teenager who's totally communicative, utterly responsible, completely dependable, and unfailingly reliable . . . why on earth didn't *you* write this chapter? After all, I'm just one of those daddies who knows a little bit about the *theory* of raising teenagers, but like so many other parents, I'm still a little puzzled by teenagers (even though I'm almost certain that once, long ago, I was one!). To me, those testy teenage years can still be a little mysterious, a little unsettling, and—for parents and kids alike—a little scary. I feel like I'm paying for my raising! My momma use to say, "When you grow up and get married, I hope you have two boys!"

Now don't get me wrong: Chad and Dusty (our two teenage superstars) are wonderful young men who certainly make Lauree and me awfully proud. But when I look out on the world that our young people have to grow up in, I must admit that I'm more than just a little bit worried.

How hard is it for a typical teenager to bump into Old Man Trouble in this crazy world of ours? Not very hard. The devil is hard at work, causing pain and heartache in more ways than ever before. And it's obvious that the devil has our young people *squarely* in his crosshairs. As Christian parents, we must remain vigilant for ourselves *and* for our kids. And when it comes to protecting our families, we need help from a full-time partner—that partner, of course, is God.

Today, as you encounter the challenges of bringing up a teenager in a difficult and dangerous world, strengthen your partnership with God through obedience, through praise, and through prayer. God is the ultimate partner, and He wants to be *your* partner in every aspect of family life. And then, if your teenage superstar does something that's a little bit wacky, remember this: There's no problem that's too big for God . . . not even those tricky teenage years.

> ℞ You know your kids are growing up when they stop asking where they came from and won't tell you where they're going.

℞ The teenage years are the times when children start trying to bring up their parents.

The reality is this—everyone is "homeschooled."
How's the school in your house?

The Swan

If you want your child to accept your values when
he reaches his teen years, then you must be worthy
of his respect during his younger years.

James Dobson

How you impress your children will be as
important as any impression that will ever
be made on their lives.

Jerry Clower

If you are in the business of affirming your teen,
you may be pleasantly surprised to hear your teen
get into the business of affirming you.

Gilbert Beers

R Entrust the raising of
your teenagers to God.
He's the only one
smarter than they are.

Don't throw away your friendship with your
teenager over behavior that has no great moral
significance. There will be plenty of real issues that
require you to stand like a rock. Save your big guns
for those crucial confrontations.

James Dobson

Preparation for old age should begin no later
than one's teens. A life which is empty of purpose
until sixty-five will not suddenly become
filled on retirement.

Arthur E. Morgan

Teenagers don't care how much you know until
they know how much you care.

Anonymous

A Teenager Is . . .

A teenager is . . . the person in your family who knows how to build a computer from scratch but doesn't know how to make up a bed.

A teenager is . . . an expert on everything *except* the things that were covered on yesterday's test.

A teenager is . . . the person in your family who has bigger mood swings than Dr. Jeckyl.

A teenager is . . . the person in your family who studies five minutes for the history exam and five months for the driver's exam.

A teenager is . . . the person in your family who never falls in or out of love more than once a week.

About the Teenage Years

The best way to keep children home is to make
the home atmosphere as pleasant as possible—and
let the air out of their tires.

Dorothy Parker

Watching your daughter being collected by her
date feels like handing over a million-dollar
Stradivarius to a gorilla.

Jim Bishop

The parents gave their daughter a new car as a
birthday present. On the windshield was a card
signed, "With all our love, Mama and Pauper."

Anonymous

Many a father wishes he were strong enough to
tear a telephone book in two, especially if he has a
teenage daughter.

Guy Lombardo

No man knows his true character until he has run
out of gas, purchased something on the installment
plan, and raised an adolescent.

Marcelene Cox

Prescriptions from Above . . .
About Our Youth

Even a child is known by his actions, by whether
his conduct is pure and right.

Proverbs 20:11 NIV

Train up a child in the way he should go, and
when he is old he will not depart from it.

Proverbs 22:6 NKJV

Children, obey your parents in all things: for this is
well-pleasing unto the Lord.

Colossians 3:20 KJV

"My son," the father said, "you are always with me,
and everything I have is yours."

Luke 15:31 NIV

You should be an example to the believers in
speech, in conduct, in love, in faith, in purity.

1 Timothy 4:12 HCSB

Dr. Swan's Prescriptions for Parent-itis

Be a parent first and a friend second: As your child grows into adulthood, you'll be tempted to become "one of the boys" (or girls). Resist that temptation. Remember that your kid has *lots* of friends but only a couple of parents. So whatever you do, don't abandon your parental responsibilities. Your teenager needs a parent more than a pal.

Have a few important rules . . . and enforce them. No matter how big they are, they still need to *abide* by your rules if they want to *reside* under your roof.

When your teenager messes up (and he will) . . . don't be too quick to bail him out. Sometimes experience isn't just *the best* teacher; it's the *only* teacher that your teenager will listen to.

Talk, talk, talk . . . and keep talking. Even if your teenager isn't too talkative, keep flapping *your* gums until he starts flapping *his*.

Chapter 11

Discipline

When I was a kid, teaching discipline to a kid was a little less complicated than it is today. Most parents figured that kids were like canoes: most easily controlled when paddled from the rear.

But today things are a little different, and there are plenty of experts who've got lots to say about teaching your kids discipline. But in the interest of time, let's cut through all the mumbo jumbo and sum everything up with a biblical truth that's as plain as the nose on my face: Discipline starts with God.

Parents who study the Bible are confronted again and again with God's intention that His children (of all ages) lead disciplined lives. God doesn't reward laziness or misbehavior. To the contrary, He expects His followers to adopt a disciplined approach to their lives, and He punishes those who disobey His commandments. So wise Christian parents teach discipline by word and by example but not necessarily in that order.

As we seek to become disciples of Jesus Christ, we should never forget that the word disciple is directly related to the word *discipline*. To be a disciple of the Lord Jesus Christ is to know His discipline.

God does not discipline out of anger, nor does He stay angry. His discipline is not like human wrath. He knows that mere weak, mortal people could not stand the blast of His divine anger. God always disciplines out of love, and as parents, we should seek to do likewise.

When you find the need to discipline your child, as you most certainly will from time to time, do so lovingly, not angrily. And remember that the greatest rewards in life usually go to the children who are lucky enough to have parents who care enough to give their kids a disciplined, loving home.

R The Bible says parents should "train up a child in the way he should go." It doesn't say, "Turn your kids over to the school system and let them train your kid in the way they think he should go."

The goal of disciplining our children is to encourage their growth as respectful, responsible, self-disciplined individuals.

Don H. Highlander

A boy or girl who knows that love abounds at home will not resent well-deserved punishment. One who is unloved or ignored will hate any form of discipline.

James Dobson

Loving discipline encourages a child to respect other people and live as a responsible, constructive citizen.

James Dobson

The alternative to discipline is disaster.

Vance Havner

℞ Discipline does not break a child's spirit half as often as the lack of it breaks a parent's heart.

Love and discipline are the foundation
of training your child.

J. Allen Peterson

Love your children with all your hearts; love them
enough to discipline them before it is too late.

Lavina Christensen Fugal

Good discipline requires time. When we have no
time to give our children, or no time that we are
willing to give, we don't even observe them closely
enough to become aware of when their need for
our disciplinary assistance is expressed subtly.

M. Scott Peck

℞ If you're unwilling to train your child in the way he should go, don't be surprised if he doesn't go there.

℞ If one examines the secret behind a championship football team, a magnificent orchestra, or a successful business, the principal ingredient is invariably discipline.

James Dobson

A Few Thoughts on Self-discipline

Without self-discipline, success is impossible. Period.

Lou Holtz

You cannot be disciplined in great things and undisciplined in small things.

George S. Patton

No horse gets anywhere until he is harnessed. No life ever grows great until it is focused, dedicated, and disciplined.

Harry Emerson Fosdick

Some people regard discipline as a chore. For me, it is a kind of order that sets me free to fly.

Julie Andrews

When we teach ourselves and our children discipline, we are teaching them and ourselves how to suffer and also how to grow.

M. Scott Peck

Prescriptions from Above . . .
About Discipline

For this very reason, make every effort to
supplement your faith with goodness, goodness
with knowledge, knowledge with self-control, self-
control with endurance, endurance with godliness.

2 Peter 1:5–6 HCSB

He who heeds discipline shows the way to life, but
whoever ignores correction leads others astray.

Proverbs 10:17 NIV

A fool rejects his father's discipline, but he who
regards reproof is sensible.

Proverbs 15:5 NASB

My son, do not despise the LORD's discipline and
do not resent his rebuke, because the LORD
disciplines those he loves, as a father
the son he delights in.

Proverbs 3:11–12 NIV

Dr. Swan's Prescriptions for Parent-itis

To paddle or not to paddle . . . that is the question: The decision is yours, but whatever you do, never paddle in anger and never *ever* do injury to a child!

Take a disciplined approach to disciplining your child: If you're too angry for your own good, put *yourself* in time-out until you can control yourself.

Be disciplined in your own approach to life: You can't teach it if you won't live it.

See as much as you can; correct as much as you should: Encouraging children to do the right thing requires an observing eye and a patient heart. Expect your children to be well behaved, but don't expect them to be perfect. In fact, an important part of parenting is knowing what to overlook and when to overlook it.

Chapter 12

Lessons about Health and Safety

*O*K, Mom and Dad, from this moment on, consider yourself officially enlisted as your family's "Chief Health and Safety Officers." It's a big job, a 24-7 job, a vitally important job, but somebody has to do it. And ultimately, that somebody is *you*—no ifs, ands, or buts.

You should begin teaching your child about health and safety long before your baby can understand what you're doing. In fact, the safety lessons should begin when you carry your newborn home from the hospital in that super-duper, ultrasafe kiddie seat. But car seats are just the beginning. As your child matures, you'll need to teach the importance of buckling up, the importance of eating right, the importance of exercising, the importance of holding hands in parking lots, the importance of staying out of the street, and a hundred other lessons too numerous to mention here. But that's just the beginning.

As your child matures, the lessons are different but no less important. At the proper time, you'll teach your kid about fire safety, bike helmets, unfriendly dogs, talking to strangers, and, once again, a hundred other lessons too numerous to mention here. But there's more.

Once your little superstar reaches the right age, you'll begin safety lectures on grown-up stuff: how to drive, whom to ride *with*, and when to get home at night (given all the tragedies that happen on the highways after midnight, curfews are a *huge* safety issue). And you'll also need to talk with your kid about the dangers of alcohol and other life-threatening drugs—not to mention a hundred other lessons too numerous to address here.

And then one day, if everything works out as you've planned, you'll have the satisfaction of knowing that your darling baby is safely past the dangers of childhood. And that's the day when you can finally pat yourself on the back and say, "Whew, I'm glad that kid has safely made it to adulthood. Being safety officer was a tough job, but it was worth it."

The End.

Almost.

You see, if you're *very* lucky, maybe *your* child will have a baby or two, so your dream of becoming a grandparent will become a reality. And if *that* happens, the training will start all over again, except this time, you'll be training the chief health and safety officers of your *precious grandbabies*. It's a big job, but somebody has to do it. And what will you teach? Hundreds of lessons . . . *far* too numerous to mention.

Safety First

A danger foreseen is half avoided.

Thomas Fuller

In everything one must consider the end.

Jean de la Fontaine

He who hesitates is sometimes saved.

James Thurber

After you've leaped, it's too late to look.

Marie T. Freeman

For safety is not a gadget but a state of mind.

Eleanor Everet

℞ If you don't take care of your body, how can you expect your body to take care of you?

Sometimes Our Kids Must Learn from Experience

Experience is a tough teacher. It gives the test
before giving the lesson.

Vernon Law

Experience keeps a dear school,
yet fools will learn in no other.

Ben Franklin

A good scare is worth more to a man
than good advice.

Edgar Watson Howe

What I like about experience is that it is such an
honest thing. You may take any number of wrong
turnings; but keep your eyes open and you will not
be allowed to go very far before the warning signs
appear. You may have deceived yourself, but
experience is not trying to deceive you. The
universe rings true wherever you fairly test it.

C. S. Lewis

Prescriptions from Above . . .

About Wisdom, Safety, and Health

The prudent see danger and take refuge, but the simple keep going and suffer for it.

Proverbs 27:12 NIV

Give instruction to a wise man, and he will be still wiser; Teach a just man, and he will increase in learning.

Proverbs 9:9 NKJV

Therefore, whether you eat or drink, or whatever you do, do all to the glory of God.

1 Corinthians 10:31 NKJV

Fear of man will prove to be a snare, but whoever trusts in the LORD is kept safe.

Proverbs 29:25 NIV

I will instruct you and teach you in the way you should go; I will counsel you and watch over you.

Psalm 32:8 NIV

Dr. Swan's Prescriptions
for Parent-itis

Thinking ahead for your child: As a responsible parent, it's up to you to use both eyesight *and* foresight. Impulsive kids, left to their own devices, tend to get themselves into dangerous situations; responsible adults, however, don't leave kids to their own devices.

Talk safety: A good way to teach safety is to talk about it *often*. The more you discuss safety with your child, the more safety conscious your child will become. Being safety-conscious means being this way *all* the time.

Adopt healthy habits inside the four walls of your home: We live in a junk-food society, but you shouldn't let your house become junk-food heaven. Make your home a haven of healthy foods. It's never too soon to teach your kid good habits . . . and that includes the very good habit of sensible eating.

Get started today: Healthy choices are easy to put off until some future date. But procrastination, especially concerning matters of personal health and safety, is foolish and worst. If you feel the need to improve the general level of your family's health, don't wait for New Year's Day; don't even wait until tomorrow. The time for you and yours to begin living a healthier life is the moment you finish reading this sentence.

Chapter 13

Taking Care of Momma (and Daddy)

Being a responsible parent requires a whole lot of energy. And that's why you and your spouse need to make certain that *both of you* keep your batteries charged.

Even the most inspired Christian parents can, from time to time, find themselves running out of stamina, and you're no exception. The demands of everyday life, combined with the stresses of raising a family, can sap your strength and rob you of the joy that is rightfully yours in Christ.

Is your energy on the wane? Are your emotions frayed? Are you a played-out parent or a sleepy-headed spouse? If so, it's time to turn your thoughts and your prayers to God. The Savior will restore your strength *if* you ask Him to. So what, dear friend, are you waiting for? God can make all things new, including you. Your job is to let Him.

Are you a tired papa who's too pooped to pop? Or are you an overworked mom who's too tuckered to accomplish your myriad of maternal duties? If so, turn your heart toward God in prayer. Then take the time—or, more accurately, *make* the time—for rest, relaxation, and reflection.

And one more thing: *please* click off that blamed TV set and start getting eight hours of sleep every night. You deserve it . . . and so does everybody else!

> Prescription for a happier and healthier life:
> resolve to slow down your pace; learn to say
> no gracefully; resist the temptation to chase
> after more pleasure, more hobbies,
> and more social entanglements.
>
> *James Dobson*

> People who cannot find time for recreation are
> obliged sooner or later to find time for illness.
>
> *John Wanamaker*

> Taking care of yourself physically really helps
> emotionally. People who get a lot of sleep, who do the
> things that relieve stress, can withstand a lot of stress.
>
> *Laura Bush*

℞   If you're sick and tired of feeling sick and tired, then you should become sick of staying up late. So do yourself a favor: go to bed.

℞ Get plenty of rest, but remember: you can never make your dreams come true by oversleeping.

Life is strenuous. See that your clock
does not run down.

Mrs. Charles E. Cowman

Take a rest; a field that has rested
gives a bountiful crop.

Ovid

Sleep is the golden chain that ties health
and our bodies together.

Thomas Dekker

Work is not always required of a man. There is
such a thing as sacred idleness, the cultivation of
which is now fearfully neglected.

George MacDonald

℞ **You cannot honor your family without nurturing your own sense of personal value and honor.**

Stephen Covey

Notice what Jesus had to say concerning those who have wearied themselves by trying to do things in their own strength: "Come to me, all you who labor and are heavy laden, and I will give you rest."

Henry Blackaby and Claude King

Some of us would do more for the Lord if we did less.

Vance Havner

Whoever you are, whatever your condition or circumstance, whatever your past or problem, Jesus can restore you to wholeness.

Anne Graham Lotz

For centuries now Christians have poured out their
hearts to the Lord and found treasured moments of
refuge.

Bill Hybels

If the pace and the push, the noise and the crowds
are getting to you, it's time to stop the nonsense
and find a place of solace to refresh your spirit.

Charles Swindoll

The amazing thing about Jesus is that He doesn't
just patch up our lives, He gives us a brand-new
sheet, a clean slate to start over, all new.

Gloria Gaither

Sometimes we need a housecleaning of the heart.

Catherine Marshall

R̸ God is not running an antique shop! He is making all things new!

Vance Havner

I wish I could make it all new again; I can't. But God can. "He restores my soul," wrote the shepherd. God doesn't reform; He restores. He doesn't camouflage the old; He restores the new. The Master Builder will pull out the original plan and restore it. He will restore the vigor, He will restore the energy. He will restore the hope. He will restore the soul.

Max Lucado

Repentance removes old sins and wrong attitudes, and it opens the way for the Holy Spirit to restore our spiritual health.

Shirley Dobson

Prescriptions from Above . . .
About Renewal

But those who wait on the LORD shall renew their
strength; they shall mount up with wings like
eagles, they shall run and not be weary,
they shall walk and not faint.

Isaiah 40:31 NKJV

And He said to me, "My grace is sufficient for you,
for My strength is made perfect in weakness."

2 Corinthians 12:9 NKJV

The inward man is being renewed day by day.

2 Corinthians 4:16 NKJV

I will give you a new heart and put a
new spirit within you.

Ezekiel 36:26 NKJV

Come to Me, all you who are weary and burdened,
and I will give you rest. All of you take up My
yoke and learn from Me, because I am gentle and
humble in heart, and you will find rest for yourselves for My yoke is easy and My burden is light.

Matthew 11:28–30 HCSB

Dr. Swan's Prescriptions for Parent-itis

It's called sleep . . . try it: If you're like most parents, you'll be tempted to try to get by on less sleep than you need. Don't do it. Go to bed in time to get the full eight hours that you need.

Sensible exercise can increase your strength: Exercise (conducted under the general supervision of your doctor) is a great way to build your energy level. An exercise program that starts slowly and builds up over time is far better than an exercise program that starts and ends quickly. Begin by walking—hopefully we can all walk and not faint.

Consider your family's healthier lifestyle a form of worship: When God described your body as a temple, He wasn't kidding. Show your respect for God's Word by keeping your temple in tip-top shape and encourage your family to do the same. Make no mistake: an important part of caring for *your* temple is getting enough rest.

Chapter 14

The Importance of Family

In a world filled with countless obligations and frequent frustrations, we may be tempted to take our families for granted. But God intends otherwise.

Our families are precious gifts from our Father in heaven. If we are to be the righteous people that God intends, we must care for our families, we must love our families, we must lead our families, and we must make time for our families, even when the demands of the day are great.

No family is perfect, and neither is yours. But, despite the inevitable challenges, obligations, and hurt feelings of family life, your clan is God's blessing to you. That little band of men, women, kids, and babies is a priceless treasure on temporary loan from the Father above. Give thanks to the Giver for the gift of family and act accordingly.

R

A family altar can alter a family.

The family is the nucleus of civilization.

Ariel and Will Durant

Children in a family are like flowers in a bouquet:
there's always one determined to face
in an opposite direction from the way
the arranger desires.

Marcelene Cox

Kids are great. They are exciting. Their potential
is simply phenomenal. And in any given family
there is the potential to change the world for God.

Maxine Hancock

Whatever the times, one thing will never change: If you have children, they must come first. Your success as a family and our success as a society depends not on what happens in the White House but on what happens inside your house.

Barbara Bush

Money can build or buy a house. Add love to that and you have a home. Add God to that and you have a temple. You have "a little colony of the kingdom of heaven."

Anne Ortland

Never give your family the leftovers and crumbs of your time.

Charles Swindoll

℞

Message to men—hold your wife and kids instead of the remote.

A family ought to be a lot more than a collection
of mutual needs. It ought to be fun.

Art Linkletter

The family: We are a strange little band of characters
trudging through life sharing diseases, toothpaste,
coveting one another's desserts, hiding shampoo,
borrowing money, locking each other out of rooms,
loving, laughing, defending, and trying to figure out
the common thread that bound us all together.

Erma Bombeck

The first essential for a happy home is love.

Billy Graham

Family faces are magic mirrors. Looking at people
who belong to us, we see past, present, and future.

Gail Lumet Buckley

℞ A child of the King
should bear a family
resemblance.

> ℞
> You know you're putting your family first when . . . your idea of a hot new car is a minivan.

Strong families are made by strong people who believe enough in the value of their parenthood that they are willing to arrange their entire lives, if necessary, around home and family.

Rich DeVos

No other structure can replace the family. Without it our children have no moral foundation. Without it they become moral illiterates whose only law is self.

Chuck Colson

The only true source of meaning in life is found in love for God and His Son Jesus Christ, and love for mankind, beginning with our own families.

James Dobson

R It takes about five years for a walnut tree to produce nuts; with the family tree, it usually takes a little longer.

Well, I hope that while I live I may keep my old-fashioned theories, and that, at least, in my own family, I may continue to feel that home is the best and happiest place, and that my son and daughter and their children will live in peace and keep from the tarnish which seems to affect so many.

Sara Delano Roosevelt

Many of the most highly publicized events of my presidency are not nearly as memorable or significant in my life as fishing with my daddy.

Jimmy Carter

Soup is a lot like family. Each ingredient enhances the others; each batch has its own characteristics; and it needs time to simmer to reach the full flavor.

Marge Kennedy

Prescriptions from Above . . .
About Our Families

These should learn first of all to put their religion
into practice by caring for their own family.

1 Timothy 5:4 NIV

Choose for yourselves this day whom you will
serve . . . as for me and my household,
we will serve the LORD.

Joshua 24:15 NIV

Every kingdom divided against itself will be
ruined, and every city or household divided against
itself will not stand.

Matthew 12:25 NIV

Love must be without hypocrisy. Detest evil; cling
to what is good. Show family affection to one
another with brotherly love. Outdo one another in
showing honor.

Romans 12:9–10 HCSB

Let love and faithfulness never leave you . . . write
them on the tablet of your heart.

Proverbs 3:3 NIV

Dr. Swan's Prescriptions for Parent-itis

God and family: Put God first in every aspect of your life. And while you're at it, put Him first in every aspect of *your family's life* too (see Joshua 24:15).

Tell the stories and write them down: The next generation won't remember the family stories they never heard, but they won't forget the ones that are written down.

A problem in the family? Talk about it! You've simply got to keep talking things over, even if it's hard. And remember: what seems like a mountain today may turn out to be a molehill tomorrow.

Don't be afraid to seek help. If you're facing family problems that you just can't seem to solve, don't hesitate to consult your pastor or an experienced counselor.

Chapter 15

Thank You, Lord, for Our Families

Every good gift comes from God. As believers who have been saved by a risen Christ, we owe unending thanksgiving to our Heavenly Father. Yet sometimes, amid the crush of life here on earth, we simply don't stop long enough to pause and thank our Creator for His countless blessings. As Christians, we are blessed beyond measure. Thus, thanksgiving should become a habit, a regular part of our daily routines.

Your family is a priceless gift from the Creator: celebrate that gift and give thanks. When you celebrate the gifts of life and love, your thankful heart will serve as a powerful blessing to you *and* to your loved ones.

Christian believers can face the demands of family life armed with the joy of Christ and the promise of salvation. So whatever this day holds for you, begin it and end it with God as your partner and Christ as your Savior. And throughout the day, give thanks to the One who created you and saved you. Place God squarely at the center of your marriage, your family, and your life. Then celebrate! God's love for you and yours is infinite. Accept it joyously and be thankful.

We never know the love of
the parent till we become
parents ourselves.

Henry Ward Beecher

Acceptance is taking from God's hand absolutely anything He gives, looking into His face in trust and thanksgiving, knowing that the confinement of the hedge we're in is good and for His glory.

Charles Swindoll

For what has been—thanks!
For what shall be—yes!

Dag Hammarskjöld

Thanksgiving is good but Thanksliving is better.

Jim Gallery

R̸
Don't have anything to be thankful for? Check your pulse!

R̥ If you pause to think, you'll have cause to thank!

Reflect upon your blessings, of which
every man has plenty, not on your past
misfortunes, of which all men have some.

Charles Dickens

Gratitude is riches. Complaint is poverty.

Doris Day

When I first open my eyes upon the morning
meadows and look out upon the beautiful world,
I thank God I am alive.

Ralph Waldo Emerson

God gave you a gift of 86,400 seconds today. Have
you used one of them to say "thank you"?

William Arthur Ward

So much has been given me, I have no time to
ponder over that which has been denied.

Helen Keller

Think of the beauty still left around you,
and give thanks.

Anne Frank

Cultivate a thankful spirit! It will be to you a
perpetual feast.

John R. MacDuff

Ironically, we often complain about the very things
that should be, if we were more honest with
ourselves, counted among our greatest blessings.

Marie T. Freeman

R℞

If you won't fill your
heart with gratitude,
the devil will fill it with
something else.

R A grateful heart can't keep complaining for long. A thankless heart can't stop complaining for long. When in doubt, choose gratitude.

Let's thank God for allowing us to experience troubles that drive us closer to Him.

Shirley Dobson

It is always possible to be thankful for what is given rather than to complain about what is not given. One or the other becomes a habit of life.

Elisabeth Elliot

God has promised that if we harvest well with the tools of thanksgiving, there will be seeds for planting in the spring.

Gloria Gaither

If you can't tell whether your
glass is half empty or half full,
you don't need another glass;
what you need is better eyesight
. . . and a more thankful heart.

Marie T. Freeman

The act of thanksgiving is a demonstration of the fact that you are going to trust and believe God.

Kay Arthur

The family circle is the supreme conductor of Christianity.

Henry Drummond

Most of us prayed that God would give us children in the first place. Then we dedicated them to Him soon after they were born. Now we need to surround them in prayer and give thanks to God for that priceless gift—our children.

Tim and Beverly LaHaye

℞ You know you're a parent when your heart is as full as your to-do list and your wallet is as empty as your refrigerator.

Prescriptions from Above . . .
About Thanksgiving

Be anxious for nothing, but in everything by prayer and supplication, with thanksgiving, let your requests be made known to God.

Philippians 4:6 NKJV

As you have therefore received Christ Jesus the Lord, so walk in Him, rooted and built up in Him and established in the faith, as you have been taught, abounding in it with thanksgiving.

Colossians 2:6-7 NKJV

Therefore, since we receive a kingdom which cannot be shaken, let us show gratitude, by which we may offer to God an acceptable service with reverence and awe.

Hebrews 12:28 NASB

And let the peace of the Messiah, to which you were also called in one body, control your hearts. Be thankful.

Colossians 3:15 HCSB

Thanks be to God for His indescribable gift.

2 Corinthians 9:15 HCSB

Dr. Swan's Prescriptions
for Parent-itis

Perpetual complaining is a bad habit, and it's contagious. . . . Make sure that your family members don't catch it from you!

Two magic words: Thank you! Your kids will never become tired of hearing those two little words, and neither will God. And while you're at it, try three more: "I love you!"

Make your feelings known: Of course you are thankful to God for all His blessings, starting, of course, with your family. Make certain your children know how you feel.

You can't count all your blessings, they're simply too many of them. But, as a Christian parent, you know where to start counting: Your Heavenly Father, His only Son, and your own children.

The Swan

Dr. Dennis Swanberg, affectionately known to his friends and fans as "The Swan," is a seasoned and solid communicator whose sly wit delivers life-enriching truths to the heart on wings of laughter.

The Swan is a highly sought after author, speaker, and TV host. He is happily married to his wife, Lauree, and is the proud dad of two boys, Chad and Dustin. He is a welcome and popular guest on Dr. James Dobson's *Focus on the Family* radio show, and his television shows have been seen by millions. He has been called "America's Minister of Encouragement" because of his constant work at lifting hearts and leading people to a richer life through his one-of-a-kind humor.

Criswell Freeman

Criswell Freeman is a doctor of clinical psychology who lives and writes in Nashville, Tennessee. Dr. Freeman has authored over one hundred books and has over five million books in print.